Dee can fix it!

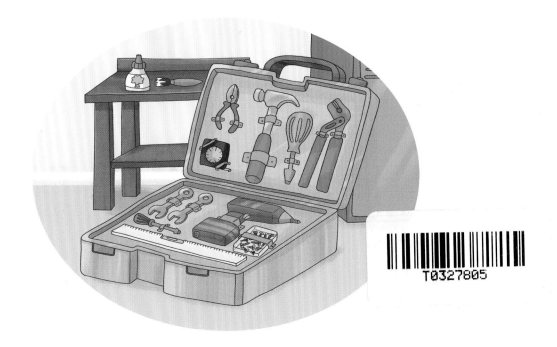

T0327805

Written by Suzy Senior

Illustrated by Sarah Lawrence

Collins

Dee can fix cars, chairs and my hair!

She keeps her tools in this silver box.

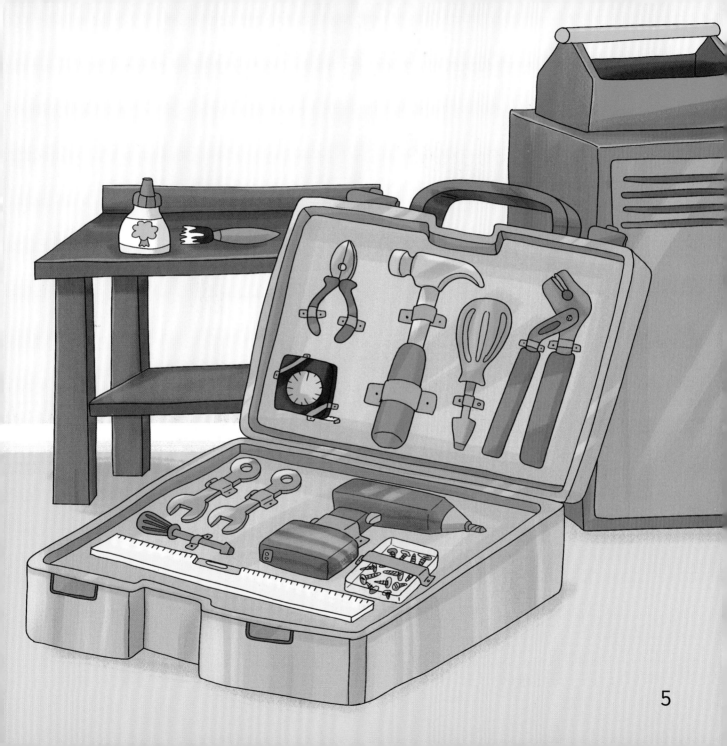

Now, she needs a hook for my rain jacket.

Dee looks in her shed.

No hooks.

She peeks right under the sink.

No hooks.

Fix it, Dee!

🐾 Review: After reading 🐾

Use your assessment from hearing the children read to choose any GPCs, words or tricky words that need additional practice.

Read 1: Decoding

- Turn to page 6. Point to **Now** and challenge children to sound out and blend. Can they identify the two letters that make one sound? (*N/ow/*) Repeat for:

  needs (*n/ee/d/s*)   **hook** (*h/oo/k*)   **for** (*f/or/*)   **rain** (*r/ai/n*)

- Encourage the children to read these pairs of words fluently, sounding out and blending in their heads.

  hair   chairs   **looks   hooks**   **needs   keeps**

Read 2: Prosody

- Turn to pages 12 and 13 and explore the punctuation together.
- Point to the exclamation mark and ask: What is this? How does it help us to read this aloud? Model reading the sentence with feeling, then let the children join in.
- Point to the ellipses on pages 12 and 13, and say: We have to pause when we see an ellipsis (three dots). Pausing makes us wait and see what happens next. Model reading the speech bubbles, then let the children join in.

Read 3: Comprehension

- Reread page 10. Point to **right**. Say: This means she looked all the way under the sink. Point to the picture and say: Dee had to take everything out to see "right under the sink".
- Focus on how the word **fix** is used in the story, using pages 14 and 15.
  - Point to the car and ask: Who fixed this? (*Dee*) Why do you think it might have needed fixing? (e.g. *maybe it wouldn't start*)
  - Ask: How does Dee fix the girl's hair? (e.g. *braiding, tying back*) Talk about how the children's hair is "fixed".
  - Open out to a discussion on what else Dee fixed and how.